T0146443

TEARS ON HER FACE

Healing the heart one poem at a time

KISHA L. PHILLIPS

TEARS ON HER FACE
HEALING THE HEART ONE POEM AT A TIME

Scripture taken from the Holy Bible, NEW INTERNATIONAL VERSION®. Copyright © 1973, 1978, 1984, 2011 by Biblica, Inc. All rights reserved worldwide. Used by permission. NEW INTERNATIONAL VERSION® and NIV® are registered trademarks of Biblica, Inc. Use of either trademark for the offering of goods or services requires the prior written consent of Biblica US, Inc.

iUniverse books may be ordered through booksellers or by contacting:

iUniverse
1663 Liberty Drive
Bloomington, IN 47403
www.iuniverse.com
1-800-Authors (1-800-288-4677)

Because of the dynamic nature of the Internet, any web addresses or links contained in this book may have changed since publication and may no longer be valid. The views expressed in this work are solely those of the author and do not necessarily reflect the views of the publisher, and the publisher hereby disclaims any responsibility for them.

Any people depicted in stock imagery provided by Thinkstock are models, and such images are being used for illustrative purposes only. Certain stock imagery © Thinkstock.

ISBN: 978-1-5320-3438-1 (sc)
ISBN: 978-1-5320-3440-4 (hc)
ISBN: 978-1-5320-3439-8 (e)

Print information available on the last page.

iUniverse rev. date: 11/22/2017

DEDICATION

I would like to thank God for giving me the gift of expression, transformation and his continuous blessings in my life. To my husband, you make me want to be a better me, I love you with my whole heart and look forward to the rest of our lives together (Persevere). To all my kids, that I birthed and the ones God has blessed me with; MWG, MP, QB, CP, BJ, SW and GG, I love all of you an thank you for the motivation you have given me to keep me striving for excellence. To all those God has placed in my life to pray for me, encourage me and push me to reach my fullest potential, thank you for your obedience. To all of you that are reading this book, know that you are worth the life you were given, be true to yourself and take inventory of your heart. Steward the relationships you have because you can't expect growth without action, lastly treat others the way you want to be treated. Blessings,

K. L. P.

It is my hopes to share my trials through my poetry, so that those who have similar situations know that there is hope. There is no fear in love. But perfect love drives out fear, because fear has to do with punishment. The one who fears is not made perfect in love. 1 John 4:18 (NIV).

CONTENTS

Lost Love

I have been exposed to a virus
That is devouring my intestines.
My organs are disintegrating, one-by-one.
I can't breathe because my lungs have deflated;
My kidneys have collapsed, and my heart has a hole in it
That can't be repaired easily.
Is it best to let me die, or wise to keep me alive?
It's a decision left up to you; you're in charge at this time.
Will your conscience bother you?
'Cause when I'm gone, you can have what was mine—
It is a treasure, for I have unconditional love.
I'm fading, and thoughts are moving quickly across my dome;
I am looking at my eyelids as my past flashes through my mind.
What is more important to you:
A true friendship that will end at an unknown time or
A love that can be rebuilt into a new relationship?
You have made your decision,
though you haven't said anything.
I feel you have failed the trust I had in you.
I have flatlined, and my body has become cold instantly because I
have died lonely.

THE ORIGINAL TEARS ON THE FACE

All smiles and laughter is not good:
Some is happiness and some is sad.
I will try to describe the feelings I have inside:
Often I'm ashamed, but it's nothing to hide.
I seem so happy, yet I am so very sad;
On the outside, I'm laughing so loud and clear,
Inside I'm crying painfully and full of tears.
I'm always reaching out to touch someone or something,
And it pulls back with a frown, not realizing that's when my tears
start coming down.
I am filled with hurt, just because I want to be loved too.
Still, my hand is pushed away. Now I'm crying, what should I do?
I do fall in love easily with a person or a beautiful object,
Such as a rose, but you still won't let me touch you,
Your heart is closed.
I'm backed deep into a corner full of fears, frightened to come out
And show you who I really am. I feel very weak and tired.
I might fall, I have to keep standing.
One day, you will realize you could have had it all.
It will be too late because I'll have gone to a safe place.
Until then, my tears will remain on my face.

I HAVE A CHOICE

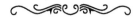

Hollow point, pointblank range to the back of the head.

Metaphorically married three years, sometimes feeling dead.

Here to listen? "Shut your mouth, you ain't got nothing to say."

Nothing important enough for me to convey, so I pray for strength; not hatred, but peace of mind

'Cause I am losing it, little-by-little, each day.

Not many pleasant thoughts left, the serpent is near. So do I destroy him or let him go his own way?

CRINGING SOUL

My skin would crawl, my body would tense up, and my heart would be full of unquestionable emotions.

You: a person like me but unlike anybody I have ever met. Why were you so angry, and sad Closed up inside, a build up of hurt that you turned into hate and discontent with the world, wanting so badly to disappear. The end couldn't come fast enough for you.

Your solution? Explosions and mental breakdowns, and no one understood why. No one understood what was happening in your life. So, you decided to make me understand your wife could have a taste of your hate. Why not? You thought. We are supposed to be one, right? Your justification for the mental torture you put me through. Me, a young woman who met a young man. Just to think: the signs were always there, I just ignored them.

We fell in love or, shall I say, lust. We got married and then the control began. I was scared, at times, to speak, trying extra hard to please, to relieve and satisfy you.

You were like Dr. Jekyll and Mr. Hyde: one day smiling with an uncontrollable laugh, the next day angry, full of rage and ready to bash something, anything. Darn, there goes the TV over the balcony. Then it was the radio. Oh, you're really mad today, let's play the guessing game. Oh why, oh why is my husband mad today? Did I burn his toast? Long day at work? Didn't laugh at his jokes? Did he lose his job? Did I work too late trying to make up for his mistakes? Is it because I wouldn't eat all my food?

Honey, I'm sorry I broke a glass. Please don't be mad.

A continuous cycle, only to find I was able to repair my scars while you made more for yourself. Now you're regretting most of your actions and amazed at how easy it seemed for me to finally let go! Blessings come from pain too. I'm at peace and being renewed daily!

CHEMICAL REACTION

You affect me like water does Alka-Seltzer; you are the fizz that comes from Pop Rocks after they hit your tongue. I know your heart is made of pure silver, but it's tarnished and needs to be polished often. You are sweet when you want to be and cold as of late. I say actions speak louder than words because I hear your words often, but your actions are blurry. You say "I love you" through the skin of your teeth as you look through me with no affection. You say "I miss you" but express negativity and vagueness in my presence, or barely even connect with me. I think you are torn between wanting the ending result and the work that it takes to get there. Our connection is being dissolved by cause and effect. When you get so far in a book you cannot unread ten chapters. I know we want a lot of the same things, but our means to an end is always a project. If we don't work together to get the correct formula, which is God, trust, honesty, love, friendship, laughter, and let's not forget communication, we will have a bad chemical reaction.

IS IT ME?

Is it me you despise as the tears fall from my eyes,
I keep wondering if it were lies you told,
To keep me in line or my hands tied.
"See, I'm here to stay" was a phrase that I heard constantly.
Until I began to believe the words that fell from your lips
Until … I believed all the words that fell from your lips—
Never doubting anything you said.
Until I put my guard down,

Is it me?
I must be tripping
Or down right slipping out of reality to have been so gullible.
I'm awake now, to never sleep so deep that I get wrapped up in this
fantasy world that I choose to be a part of.

Disappointment blows through the air once
Again!

SELF-LOVE

Being alone makes you understand the purpose of self-love.
This world is a very cruel place to be in with an unstable mind-set.
If you have a lot of time on your hands, you may use that
time to think—the negative thoughts are there.
You don't have to be an evil person to experience injustice.
Satan can seem powerful and, without the
right one on your side, God,
You don't have a chance.
So, remember: no one else is obligated to love you.
How could you expect someone to love you
if you don't even love yourself?
Although it happens.

YOU

Inside, I know you're mine—I would love to believe that,
But life has no guarantees, so all I basically have are my hopes and
dreams.
You are as beautiful as the moonlight and as real as the evening stars.
Gentle and loving, sincere beyond limit, you are my unspoken secret
That I cannot keep to myself; you are my happiness that I have
hungered for, for so long. You say "I'm here to stay"—that is a promise
that you cannot keep.
Plans have setbacks all the time, unintentionally. It's unpredictable as
of now.
I can only take one day at a time and hope you'll be here with me
forever.

MOTHER

You mean the world to me;
I am proud to have you near.
I can count on you to evaporate my tears,
brighten my days, and erase most of my fears;
You restore my courage and energize my soul.
You have taken a big step in life
To make your future bright and shade out the old.
You have done a good job raising the three of us,
Even though we made such a fuss.
As a young mom, you did the best you could with the knowledge that
was on
Display.
I carry you with me throughout each day,
Knowing you are watching over me, proud of my accomplishments
as you
Always made it known. I can hear you in Heaven saying that's my
baby.
I love you and miss you so much Mom, I will continue to make you
proud; you're still my Shero …
Rest in Paradise Mom (E.W.).

UNLIMITED

Who has control? Is it the man?
Or is it my man? Is it me? Or is it Sam?
See, I'm not talking about Uncle; I'm taking about my dad.
Yeah, his birth name is Sam too.
Did he make me who I am today?
If I would have known him,
Do you think my whole life would have had a delay
A slight twist or change? I have damaged brain cells,
So I am a bit deranged … it is correctable though
With the right amount of love and the right person
Me and my heavenly father!
I need to learn to love myself—feed, nourish, pamper, and
Live according to my purpose and the will of God for my life..

I KEEP STANDING

Empty: a feeling you swallow and keep right on going.
Something that gets you down but gives you a whole new perspective on life.
Problems that bring tears to the eyes, but you're too proud to let them fall.
Anxiety that builds up, but you're too smart to let it spill.
Loneliness that grows, but you're too modest to cry for a friend's ear.
Hungry for happiness, but you'd rather starve than ask for a spoonful of love.
And punishment that makes you start all over again.

Rainy Tear Drops

Tears that fall without warning.
I want to be strong, but I always feel like mourning.
The sadness is thick, and it comes once or twice a day.
I'm seriously wondering how to get away
Not physically, but mentally.
Thinking hard about a plan to dismiss the tears I develop
From my plans, job, family, and friends.
I have a slight problem that gets very hard to mention:
I get distressed if I don't have your love and attention
Something that is not understood
Unless,
The tables are turned. If you're put second I'm often burned.
It will take time for my lonesome fears to stop
Until then, there will be many of those rainy tear drops.

BLAME

Who has your mind? Are you in control of your thoughts?
Is it pity you sought when you tried to carry the world on your
shoulders?
And when you fall down—whose fault it that?
Not mine, Sam's, your parents'—darn!
No worthwhile opportunities …
What has that done to me?
Cheated me or corrupted my capacity of my learning abilities?
Gifts will eventually dissolve if not used.
I've been given a chance to enhance my gifts from the Almighty
Which will be such a sight to see.
So, if I lose out, I can only blame
Me.

I Wish I Were Your Queen

Your queen is white, brown, and green. And when she is happy, she
turns red.
Nothing could ever take the place of your queen.
If someone tries to take her, you get mean.
You spend so much time with your queen.
You would do almost anything for her;
You treat her nice, hold her tight, but caress her gently.
You spend so much money on your queen.
Better believe your queen is clean.
You keep her warm; she has a beautiful shape.
She has her own room, and you keep her groomed.
You'd travel across the world
Anywhere she is, you're going.
She says, "Jump," and you say, "How high?"

When are we going to wake up, to this reality and receive our
inheritance? Straddling the fence is not the way, of the worlds
influence and corrupted capability.
We idolize, worldly possessions as though they will be here forever
We seek happiness and joy within our reach. I am glad to admit, I
don't have to be your queen, instead it's enough for me to be a princess
and serve a mighty King.

LONGING FOR SOMETHING PERMANENT

As I look out to the ocean, I see the moon reflect from the waters,

A line that leads me to the light,

A feeling of an untouchable moment.

As waves ripple down the sea,

I think of you without closing my eyes.

I see your face and smile and hear your laughter.

As birds fly by, I experience peace within my inner spirit...

Lights so bright I need sunglasses to see.

Just as quickly as I turn, darkness overpowers my world.

It's everlasting. I can feel you trying to reach me, but you are far away.

I see images of your home here on earth,

But the overcast weather brings out shadows from the mountains.

Will what we have take a toll on all unimportant things?

Well, we have become one and made a bond, will we be forever as

long as forever is?

I have made a discussion, that you are here to stay. Let the

transformation begin. I receive you as my Lord and Savior.

I Cherish You

You are a friend I can trust with my own.

You comfort my unhappiness; you don't leave me all alone.

I get headaches when I think about you not being here one day,

So won't you look me in the eye and tell me you're here to stay?

I told you before: you don't have to be alone to be lonely.

Taking a friend is your way of controlling;

Having a true friend is hard to come by.

Once you cross the line, you can't turn back the hands of time.

So, I say again, it's all up to you:

Do you want an everlasting friend or a sky that is sometimes blue?

SMILES

How likely and beautiful
Just comforting
More happiness
Teeth, beautiful teeth
A smile with dimples
And cute with freckles
A thought of Spreckles
A theater where shows are put on
And laughs are belted out
Laughs...
Where there are laughs
There are smiles
Big smiles
Little smiles
Round smiles, and
Proud smiles

Be Thankful

We often complain about abuse
And deny the things you have given us.
So selfish that we take, take, take
And very seldom give.
My Almighty has given me life!
The breath I breathe, Oh Lord, it's in need;
The sight I see, you have given to me;
My nose and smile,
Teeth so I can eat,
Sense of touch
Oh, Lord, you are too much.
A big, beautiful heart comes from up above.
The long legs and feet to walk,
I can't forget my voice to talk.
There is much more I can't begin to mention
You have also given me trust, to have faith in you and
The changes you guide me to do.
My heavenly Father, I just want to say:
Thank you!

LOVE

Love will make you blind
Love will make you get played
Love sure as heck hurts
Love can make you feel like dirt
Love is thick like cement
It will have you missing many events
Love is expensive like diamonds
Love will have you climbing
Love is full of excuses
Love will have you accepting abuse
Love will make you die
Because being in love can be full of lies
The lies of the enemy, as he gets you to believe the emotions you are
feeling are love,
Well it isn't and it can't be.
True love is perfect and can only come from a
Perfect place, I am blessed to have finally found love.

GIVE ME A SOLUTION

You are feeding my insanity with your anger and jealous ways.

You can't tell me different, I can hear when you lay

Because you speak in your sleep; the hatred and evil demons eject

from your soul.

I know you are out for revenge

Disrespectfulness bleeds from your skin.

Love me, but what does that mean to you?

I have to know it means, I have your back,.

Never because of selfishness.

I'm starting to recognize the cycles.

It's not okay though you may like to believe so, and though I don't

want to, I may have to go.

It's a continuous pattern: my heart is shattering when you do the

things you do

Almost to the point that I feel lower than dirt.

As I write this poem, my tears are flowing

I don't know for how long

What I do know is that I will be blessed

With the Lord's happiness!

Beauty Is Only Skin Deep

So it is said:
Beauty reflects from within a person,
Ejected by his or her personality.
You can only determine whether a person's beauty is real
Through conversation.
His or her outer beauty doesn't matter; it just helps when it comes to a
relationship.

DEATH WITHIN

My soul is damaged, almost beyond repair.
You're angry with me—how could you dare?
I thought you cared.
I'm looking for happiness,
Do you think there is such a thing?
I thought that was the reason you gave me this ring—
It was the beginning of a new paradise,
Sunshine and sunset more than once, we seem to forget
our main purpose; or it's just easier to quit.
I don't have the answers to all your questions.
So, when you ask, don't expect the perfect response
Because I don't have it rehearsed.
Try to remember that, when you pressure me, I am bound to burst
into a rage
'Cause now I'm mad...
You have crossed the line
I asked you to stay behind.
We continue to hurt each other; it is now a trend.
And it's much too late: Because I'm dying within.
Lord, unscramble my heart!

ALIVE

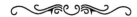

Fresh air blows through me as the Almighty God feeds thee.

There's joy within my heart and bones because I know that I am not alone.

Tender kisses of his grace and favor strengthen my soul,

Heating my insides that once were cold.

Watching over his foundation,

He nurtures me from the inside out

With priceless gifts of the mind.

To be patient, and kind

To spend time with you feels new, so what would you do?

Continue on the right path or go backwards because its easy and brings pleasure

It's the key to happiness but not joy, and it will cause you not to be blessed.

You're dead for so long; then you find a place where you belong.

These are decisions only you can make.

Can One Person Make a Difference?

If you feel something is not right,

Not going the way it should,

Sometimes you might hesitate to speak out.

You figure, who is going to listen to me?

Well, if you don't speak out, no one is going to listen.

You'd be surprised what one can do.

You may not change the problem or everyone's perspective on the situation,

But you can make a difference.

Martin Luther King Jr. made a difference; he had a dream.

His dream came true, though he wasn't exactly sure what would happen.

He risked his life to have peace,

To end racism.

He might not have completely changed these problems,

But that one man made a difference in a lot of our lives.

Happy True Day,

Martin Luther King Jr. and family.

It's Okay to Love

Your smiles, your laugh:
So sincere, so sweet.
Your touch, your kiss:
So lovely, so deep.
Your voice, your heart:
Don't worry it's all right.
Just hold me:
I'll squeeze you so softly, so tight.
I'm here always
Let our friendship grow,
become strong and intact.
We are here now, so don't ever look back.
I promise I'll be true,
It won't be a show,
So please, my love, don't ever let go!

CAN YOU HEAR ME

I'm talking to whomever is listening; sometimes I need an ear too.

So, what do you want me to do?

I'm a human being; far from immortal.

I've been talking for a long time now, and not yet have I gotten a response.

Maybe I'm the only one on Earth still alive.

It was quite the same when I was a little girl: whenever something was on my mind,

I would try and talk about it, but no one was ever listening,

So I would talk to myself, like I am now—does that make me crazy?

Now I keep things to myself, I guess because no one else listens.

I'm a great listener, too; it means a lot to a person like me.

Excuse me, what did you say?

"Huh", can you hear me?

BLOODSHED

Screams from the mental
Psycho, but gentle.
Worries of the mind, incomplete and kind,
Heartbreaks, from untrusted love friends.
Unsafe secrets with an extended hand.
Who do I turn to? Definitely not you.
I can't talk and have you listen without feeling blue.
The heart hurts more than often
But what's worse is: my only good friend
Is my book and pen!

THOSE EYES

Hypnosis
Under a spell that can't be broken
On cloud nine when you look at me
Those eyes
Millions of words being said
Without your lips moving
Drawing me into your zone
Wow, I would like to be all alone with you
To just stare into your eyes
Those eyes
Like being hooked
Oozing through my being
You know you're making me crazy see,
I can't concentrate enough to fight it
'Cause you're melting me
As you look at me with those eyes.

WHY NOT LET GO

Full of hate that hate made
Is it that you're just afraid?
I'll be gone soon one day
Remember away doesn't have to be physically
Mentally I'm already fading
In my new home, I received lots of shade, rest, and encouraging
thoughts
That is the only thing that keeps me alive
Closing my eyes and dreaming of my new home!
God please keep me strong.

WOMAN

A unique foundation
Strong impact on one's life
Heroic figure, downloaded into her DNA Nothing can penetrate her
walls or light
Will live without for her child to eat right
Will be stern with him or her
To learn about him or her
This woman listens to you when you have
No one else
She'll love you no matter what flaws you may have
No matter what you believe in
Whether or not you sin
This woman will comfort, shelter, and protect
There is only one thing she wants in return:
Respect!

TRUE FRIEND

You are the only one that makes me happy when I am sad
You seem to be the only one that calms me down when I am mad
You help magnify my love for myself and others
You seem to give me fresh air when I am smothered
You are the one that enhances my beauty in my own eyes
I never have to worry about you telling me lies
Sometimes I wonder why you're so special to me
I think being truthful is the key
If only I could turn back the hands of time
My best friend could be all mine
But I'm grateful to have you as a true friend
'Cause we have something special
I wouldn't want to end
Best friends forever.

ENDLESS

As pure as my breast, you seem to confess how evil the world is.
From the time I rise to the moment I recline to rest, my heart
existence.
As I lie in bed, gazing into the darkness,
I gather many thoughts (positive and negative),
I love those who love me my friends and family.
And I hate double standards, revenge, selfishness, and slavery.
At times, depression is uncontrollable.
I try to think of a reason to go on living,
Continue my life.
Emptiness causes sorrow and gloom.
I try to rebuild my self-esteem.
My life has had a pattern from the time I was a child.
It goes on forever without change.
I continue to wonder whether my hollow personality is
Deranged.

IMPRISONMENT

Screaming as the walls close in on my mental
Locked out of a life I was sure was mine
Trapped in hatred and misery
Forced to be blind in situations that far incline
Toward your opinions and opportunities
Helpless against man-made rules
Only enforced when convenient
Overlooked when you want to be lenient
My heart is burning with desires that I can't fulfill
I was taught my feelings are unreal
I cry louder inside my heart while being overlooked by people
around me
I deal with problems that might appear in their path
I finally realize this is nothing but the evil ones laugh

LIFE, WHAT IS IT

You and I:
It is a privilege that we seem to take for granted.
In this, you can find happiness
Understand it comes from within.
Enjoy your life
'Cause death eventually follows.
Life is planned before your time;
It's quite complicated, so you have little control over it.
Life can be slavery of the mind;
You can get lost and be hard to find.
You can develop lives with a man and a woman.
Be wise, like a baby as it opens its eyes.
Life is hard, unfair, and short;
Life is easy, exciting, and natural;
Life is what you make it!
Make sure you build a solid foundation.

RELIEVED

A moment of fresh air completes my attitude
So I feel relieved
An uncontrollable laugh is comforting
So I feel relieved
A compliment out of the blue is flattering
So I feel relieved
A sparkling look is warm
So I feel relieved
To solve a problem with a reasonable answer
Makes me feel relieved
To finally open up to a listener instead of a talker
Makes me feel relieved

TEARS ON THE FACE

As you look at me and see my smile,

It sort of looks like when I was a child.

I remember looking at an old photo.

All I saw was this place and, surely, there were tears on my face.

When all the other children where happy,

I was in this deep, dark dump, searching for something that has never

sunk in:

An imaginary friend, a favorite toy, real joy,

Attention from my mother, a hug from my brothers,

Anything I could find,

A visit from my father.

Well, it never happened enough, so I tried to become tough

And confide in myself. Then I ran out of breath.

I could never hold up or erupt.

I have many scars, mentally,

That I just can't ditch, so you call me a witch.

Well, hurt me more, that is how you score.

Tears come so natural to me;

That's how I release my steam.

I hope I'm never misplaced,

Yet and still, there will always be tears on my face.

DYING WHILE ALIVE

Constant cries
Tears falling
Head pains growing
Heartache forming as my insides are storming
Walking to the end of time
Not caring but daring life's situations
Eager to leave with no preferred destination

THE KEY

Hurt is in my heart and it is hard to explain.

I don't know why it's there and won't go away.

Temporary relief is all I receive.

Just now, the ideal of happiness strikes my brain.

Is being alone my destiny? Should I get used to being my own company?

When you are as strong minded as I am,

A big change is hard to adjust to, but I'm willing.

If it means the luxury of many burdens lifted from my soul.

I have yet to find the key that opens the door to happiness.

Or am I just not ready?

God is the key!

IT'S MINE

Have you ever been so afraid to take something you knew was
rightfully yours?
You have a 50/50 chance, either way it goes.
Use confidence and take your prize, it will most likely be in your
favor.
To grab that prize and have the look of uncertainty upon your face
Will cause there to be a price you have to pay.
So I'm not conceited,
I'm convinced as I walk away with my
Prize!

Just for You Because I Understand

Is this a cry of relief or
Are these tears of grief
That I have so frequently?
When will it all stop?
Is this a dream someone is having?
Will they wake up and we'll all just disappear?
Will everything just drop?
It seems as if someone has opened me up
And poured sour milk into my veins
Yes, it does sound a bit strange, but I hurt
And I'm so tired of doing it alone,
With no one to share the good and the bad.
Somehow, I know it will not end this way,
So I stand back and look into the mirror and I see you.
I understand you're just tired,
We are tired, but we can share our burdens

LOVE IS AN ACTION

The feelings you have could be very strong,
But love is what you do, not how you feel.
Because feelings can be deceptive,
Lust can disguise itself,
You can lust for someone one day
And tomorrow have no interest in that person.
It's easy to say
I love you,
But to show love has many steps and takes time.
Love is complicated and has many consequences,
So think twice before you say you love someone.

Definition of a Man

A man will look you straight in the eyes while talking to you
A man is honest with his woman and himself, regardless of the
Consequences
Never is he afraid of comments and their true meanings
A man has room for positive changes
And learns from his mistakes
A man encourages compromise in his relationship
A man avoids macho comments and embarrassing his woman in the
presence of others
A man goes the extra mile to please or make his woman happy
Knowing she will do the same
A man loves his woman unconditionally
A man never makes promises he cannot keep
A man takes care of his family the best way he knows how
The rest of you are only males

I Can Fly

As I spread my wings,
The wind carries me.
I glide through the air
And I feel so free.
My heart is finally content because
I'm ready for the Lord.
I'm tired of this selfish world, because it has left me unhappy and I
am bored.
I finally understand my life has been planned from beginning to
the end.
I will now practice patience and know that all things happen in his
timing.
As I live to serve him, I claim my inheritance, spread my wings
and fly.

"531992 A Teens Heart"

You will realize when it's gone
Every day goes by and it will get a little harder
I'm curious if you just forgot or don't care anymore
I can admit now that I have made some mistakes but
I can accept them
All I have now is the memories you told me not to forget
What we had was potential true love ready to grow but
When you have something good you think it's not true
Or you don't want it until it's too late
I'm happy for your ambition, success, and eagerness
I'm proud of your dreams you are making come true
I just need you to know that I still love you!

I Am a Rose

I am so beautiful; I reach for the sky.

Bright as the shining sun,

Glowing like the candles of love

With the fragrance that makes you eager to experience love.

With the secret to live and have everlasting life,

My love is for an eternity; my body is as strong as the thorns that are
bittersweet.

Hurts to the touch but protects the very beauty that must be
preserved.

I am a rose.

I am learning to guard my heart.

I Know You Are with Me Always

I know that you love me;
It brings security.
Knowing you'll never leave me
Shows me you are true to thee.
Remembering the Golden Rule
"I will always love you" brings a smile to my face,
Comfort through the soul that no one can erase.
Thank you, Almighty Father.

BLANK PAGE

Sitting here looking at my page with nothing on it
Mind blank but moving a million miles a minute
The body motionless, still as if I were the Statue of Liberty
So as not to let any emotions pass through me
Feeling everything, unable to express something, one thing, anything.
Motionless, loneliness, experienced wanting more, not a meaningless
Relationship
Complications for the duration of a month or a year
How do you weed through the impure ones?
Hundreds in line, but no one has the time to, or wants to, make the
Effort to be real with themselves
It's all about the skrill, cheddar, and money
So we often act ill and end up lonely because we can't even be true with
Ourselves
Life is short and you only have one; being honest starts with yourself.
Don't pass up a good thing, good things are hard to come by.

BLOOD ON THE BRAIN

I get headaches often, migraines.

Feels like my head is bleeding inside.

They started years ago, abuse, disappointment, and tears I don't know

For the most part, I feel it is caused by stress

If I don't feel it in my brain, then I feel it in my chest, in the form of a heartache

I used to be a careless person, and now I can say I am careful about what I say or do

I find myself stressing about work, home, my family, good health, my mother, my mother's addictions, conflicts, and homelessness

I'm one person and I have dreams that I have yet to fulfill or attempt to make real

The solution is simple, I need to be still, let go and let God, and stop trying to do things in my own will.

How Could You

Love me? How could love live in that heart of stone?

You want me to hold you, but you tell me to leave you alone.

You said I don't talk to you, but your ears are closed.

Don't you think that is strange? Or is that the promise you said: you'll change?

Not long ago, you made all these promises—to whom?

It doesn't matter, because I can't think of one you have stayed true to.

Faith in You

No wall is high enough
No trees tall enough
No mountains wide enough
To block your truth from my soul
So much sealed within my heart, I know at the hardest times you are
right here with me
Walking, running, reading, writing, listening with me
Building me up to stand as tall as your kingdom, your castles
Dealing with the hassles of everyday life
I know you are here to hold, mold, and teach (not preach), so I
unleash my soul to you!
Father, I come to you as a living sacrifice.

BORN AND DELIVERED TO THE SAME

Born to a quick tempered woman who's been through a lot of caution and danger signs in her life, danger—handling them the best way she knew how but, at times, her anger was overwhelming, forcing her to say things she often regretted.

Tears she held back to show her strength

Things she did without to show her love

Unconditionally holding a place in her heart for her seeds, yet saying hurtful things to make my soul bleed

Not understanding it was affection, I was in need

Of guidance and knowledge

Of the truth how to become a woman

Instead, she taught me what I saw in her everyday life and I learned her interpretations of how to be a wife

Although she warned me about being ready, I ignored her advice because to me I was a lady

I had not been given a father, unfortunately, so I looked to her for male qualities

At a young age, I fell in love at least my definition of "in love"

Yet, the only thing I needed was from up above

In my remembrance, I was blind, now I hurt knowing I can't turn back the hands of time

I am forever going forward; nothing in me will ever be ashamed of my past, only learned lessons and remembering how I was born and delivered to the same

THE WORLD WE LIVE IN ...
MY PRAYER TO THEE

The world we live in is coming to an end
Waiting for us to break down in the dust we came from
Holding on, I am, because the Lord nourishes my body, keeping me
strong and able to fight off the forces that live within my household
God, I pray to you: kill the chills within me that are caused by the
serpent, wanting me to become
part of his gang I will not
I will not be shaken, I will not be shaken
I will rise to the top, I will strive to live a righteous and everlasting
life
My prayer
In this letter Lord, I write to you to speak it out loud and put it to
truth
I need strength, so will you walk with me?
I need your love, so will you hold me?
I need happiness, so will you teach me?
I need to be righteous, so will you mold me
To be the one you need me to be?
O, Lord, I see thee
O, Lord, I breathe thee and, most of all, I do need thee to help me be
the one you need me to be
I am calling, calling your name, my Lord
Will you speak to me until I hear thee?

TRUE LOVE

Truth, sincerity, and silence
Love is forever, and if you believe you have ever been in love (true
love), you wouldn't be able to explain clearly how you felt completely
Just somewhat, like broken English
In a literature class, all you know is you'd do anything for that special
person and nothing to harm them. There's a feeling of a hatching
cocoon and hummingbirds in the stomach, cloud nine in the mind,
unlimited smiles across your face, staring contests for hours, never
speaking from the mouth but knowing exactly what the other is
thinking, knowing you'd give anything without a second thought for
that person.
Now that's love. I love you C. D. P.
You are the King of my Dreams

A Father Is Special

A father is special, sort of like a best friend
You know he's not going anywhere because he's there until the end
Supportive, comforting, even soothing when I was about to cry, he
made me understand that I could talk to him about anything and
never have to lie
He teaches me about life, plays with me at the park, and loves me
with all his heart
Even if he tells me no, I know he cares forever
So I will be his princess, and I never want my dad to be sad—you see,
I love him, and dreamed about being his little princess every day. I
daydreamed of all the fun things he would teach me, it just took 30
years for us to actually meet.

INDEPENDENCE

Off to peace and quiet, a new life
As a woman, not a wife.
Sanity, fresh air, and new ideas.
A new beginning as a strong individual.
Steps and goals toward happiness,
My time is now and where the Lord places me.
Time to face thee with my palms up and open,
Waiting to receive my blessings.
Yes, Lord, I hear you, and I know you hear me calling out your name.
As I walk toward the light, I'm as calm as a newborn in its mother's
arms
Because I know, soon, things will be right. At first it all didn't make
sense, now I understand that this is my chance for real independence.

HEALING

I am overwhelmed by the emotions in my heart.
Happiness and completion.
I can't tell them apart, wanting it all
From the end to a fresh start
Attention, center of attraction, and
Compliments from the heart.
Do I ask for too much?
High maintenance, like a brand new car,
Mood swings from out of nowhere.
I want to be held and caressed
With tender love and care.
No questions asked, a feeling all in one.
Knowing what I long for,
Sometimes you give too much space
at the wrong time.
Will I ever feel complete or will I always be a part of a piece of pie
that someone ate?

DESTINY

I often wonder what my destiny is.
Is this it? Is this the extent of it all?
Or is this the first step of my happiness?
I'm standing at the end of this tunnel, it seems so long.
Never-ending. But at the end of this tunnel is a bright gleam of light,
energy that fills my entire body, giving me faith, ensuring me this is
just the beginning of a good thing.
My destiny.
I will continue to strive forward, enduring into the Lord's will for me,
Because, it is my destiny.

To All My Mothers

I know the last days have been hard

It is only a test, so please don't disregard the love, or the promises,

He has given to us who believe in Him guarantees you will be
blessed.

So, in the morning when you rise and in the evening when you close
your eyes, never forget He's there and will never leave your side as
long as you try to abide by the rules He has set.

This too shall pass, and don't you ever forget.

I love the three of you, for all that you have imparted in me (E.W.,
D.C., and R.E.).

Your daughter,

K.L.P.

TO MY LOVING KIDS

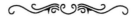

McKenzie, you make me laugh, you make me cry.

You don't even know or understand, but I would die for you if I had to.

You are a miracle only God could create.

I prayed early and you came late, later in life when God knew I would be rid of selfishness and ready for you.

I look at you and you are still a dream to me one from which I never want to wake.

To hear you say the words, forming them with your young mouth, I'm so amazed. Your actions are advanced, and I feel joy when I see you dance.

Happy feet and expressions that bring me such joy, happiness can't even measure up.

MSWG, you are the best thing that ever happened to me. I love you with my whole heart.

Miranda, you are an answered prayer and by the faith of your big sister, you are here.

You give me laughter, you give me tears, you give me smiles, you bring me fears.

For you to be such a small package you carry a grand presence, demanding the attention when you enter a room.

The love you share with us is displayed in so many ways, from the squeeze of daddy's nose to you laying your head on his chest, to the love in your little voice as you say mom as your arms wrap around my neck, to the wet kisses on my cheek, as you strike a pose in my shoes like mama look, I'm on fleek.

From the looks you give your brothers when they have you in their arms, or your screeching laugh while playing with your sister. You are so full of the love that we can't get enough of, you are our own angel from up above.

Quentin,

As tears fill my eyes, they are happy tears, I am so grateful to have you in my life. I knew you were sent from God in my life to start my transformation from bad to good. You were my sign from God to show me that I could have love in my life and that it really does exist here on earth.
Though I am not the mom who gave you birth, I love you with my whole heart and plan to be here throughout your entire life to watch you grow into the man God has called you to be. I am so proud of you.

Cordon,

I hope you know that you are special to me and I believe in you and the man you are growing into.
Although your personality is reserved, I know that you have dreams to fulfill as you are still figuring them out yourself.
I have seen you grow and develop into a young man, I am proud to call you my son. Continue to learn and believe in yourself, know that it is a process we all go through. You are such a gifted young man, don't give up on these gifts for you were meant to share them with the world.

Love, Mom

My ADD Will Be the Success of Me

My ADD will be the success of me. How do I figure this?

My mind never stops thinking, moving, syncing

With the gifts that were instilled in me at birth by my Father.

Before birth—conception—the direction in which I wanted to move was forward, straight ahead—not backward. But the calculation is a confusing math problem that I can't figure out. It's like numbers and symbols all over the page, but what formula do I use? Did I fall asleep in class on that day? I look at my notes and come up with nothing. Is the answer right in my face and I need to put on my glasses?

All of these talents I have, yet I don't know where to begin. It's hard to breathe—not because I don't have oxygen, but because there is a kink in the tube that leads to my lungs.

Feeling the pressure in my chest, I think of my daughter who hangs from my breast as she nurses to get the nutrients and energy she needs. So how do I get the energy I need? From God, her, and myself.

So, as I take a step back, put on my glasses, breathe, fall to my knees, and put my nose to the floor, I exhale and tears fall rapidly from my eyes because God is whispering in my ear Jeremiah 29:11-13. He is saying that He is here for me and will never leave me—nor has he failed me yet. He knows the desires of my heart and He shall fulfill them as He sees fit. "Just use and exercise the gifts I have given you," He says.

Not all at once will it happen, so I will take baby steps, take my time, focus, and know it's okay that my ADD will be the success of me!

DADDY'S LITTLE GIRL

You are my angel, my sweet, the blood that pumps through my heart.
I cried like a baby when we were blessed with you. Even as little
as you were, you had the superior presence of the princess you are.
Although I am supposed to be tough, the man of the house I am.
When I look at the sparkle in your eyes as you say "Daddy's home," I
melt. Then I am reminded that you are the boss. It always brightens
my day when you read me a story, draw me a picture, dance with me,
play-fight or wrestle. Most of all, I love when we say our prayers at
night. Every father hopes for a son, but you know what, baby girl,
I am so glad that I have you because I have the best of both worlds.
I can still teach you to skip rocks, climb trees, and play sports, but,
each morning when you sit down for Daddy so I can comb your hair
or get you dressed for the day, you are teaching me how to be the
best father I could have ever prayed to be. You are growing so fast.
Seems like just yesterday when I cradled you in my arms; now I give
you piggyback rides. Soon, I will be dropping you off at grade school,
wiping your tears from a broken heart, and then walking you down
the aisle after mommy gives you a set of her pearls. But, for now and
until forever, I will cherish each day with you. Now and even then,
you will always be Daddy's little girl. I love you, baby.

Love,
Daddy

My Letter to God

Hello Father,

It's me again. I know you are probably wondering what I want now. Well God, you have answered so many of my prayers. I have been loved and married. And I'm praying for at least one last chance to be a wife. I can wait though.

Let me clear my throat and wipe the smile from my face because I am smiling. I figured I have cried for so long and, since you have blessed me with beautiful teeth and a cute face, I can at least be grateful. Oh, I'm sorry, my ADD has kicked in once again.

So, back to what I was saying: my daughter, I love her so much, sometimes it's hard to focus on what I want to do, teach, and show her. It's hard to make sure it's what you want me to do.

She is so funny God, but her love is so powerful and fulfilling. Then Lord, there is my brother, he has come around to rebuild his relationship with you, and he's so happy about it that he can shout it from the rooftop. Then there's my other brother, who now doesn't hesitate to use the word Mom as he sings her happy birthday in his Barry White voice (okay, Barry Manilow). Yes Lord, these are happy tears.

My mom, well she is very complex, but you know that already. If someone takes the time to know her and doesn't mistake her motives, they would learn that she is funny, loving, smart, and somewhat of a SuperShero. She will always find a way to save the day. Then there is my grandma, I'm grateful for her deliverance, and all her prayers.

My heavenly Father, I thank you for my strength and understanding, the love of my extended family, my heart, and the ability to pay it forward.

Your Daughter,

K.L.P.

PAIN AND PLEASURE

As I feel your pleasure, I see your pain.

Looking into your eyes, your soul is revealed to me.

Disappointment after disappointment and broken promises;

Years of tears, fears, screams, and barely any cheers.

Feeling at fault to some degree (and thinking you may also agree)

Walls up like dams, layers of brick, thick as you, dismissed just as quick.

Not trying to hear the nonsense you bring, .

Tired of being used and abused overworked and underpaid is an understatement.

Just plain tired of the hand you have been dealt, yet understand the blessings you receive when the time is right, like your little twin; your bread and butter; the rock that doesn't even touch the net, yet it's in: swish.

If I could, I would make all the bad go away, and give you all the joy you deserve.

CHANGE

Change begins with you
In life, love, forgiveness, and most things you do.
I had to come to the reality that I can't control others' actions or their
Thoughts. I can only control my own toward others, though cause and
effect can make the difference between positive action or negative
clashing.
We have to be real with ourselves and think out a situation before
acting on the right here and right now. Men and women are
emotional creature's women more than men, but some women have this
fairytale way of thinking: it will be just as perfect
In the end as in the beginning. The relationship will change, we need
To change with it. As long as we are being real with ourselves, we can
Realize it's about compromising to keep the relationship going and
keeping God first!
When you take two adults and put them together, they have to learn
each other in a living environment and communicate their likes and
dislikes. At the beginning, it might be a little strange, but keep in
mind there is nothing wrong with a little change.

My Tears Are My Liquid Prayers

Lord,

I wonder how much more I can take. You took the man I love, and though I wasn't mad at you, he was my best friend, partner, and love. I wasn't ready for him to go; now I am left to raise our son into a man. At first I wasn't sure I could go on, but this is your plan for me, and this I know. It is the times when I am alone that I get scared and lonely, but I know I have to stay strong because you are here with me (so I am definitely not alone). The Devil pulls at my heartstrings, whispering that I am defeated. He is a lie. I am strong. Through Christ, I will not be cheated out of the journey you have set me on, the journey that allows me to move forward with the love and support that is evident with all of its vibrant presence: my girls, my sisters, my family, and my friends. This is the beginning of a rebuilt strength, nowhere near the end. I know these tears form in my eyes and fall down my cheeks. In those moments, I am drained, I am weak, but the tears evaporate into prayers. With my tongue, I speak the words in my heart, mind, body, and soul. I thank you, I love you, and, through you, I am strong!

TORN OR BORN

Back and Forth like tug-a-war'ing with the enemy about spiritual Dedication, obligation, to those my father places in my life to encourage, pour into and I'm here worrying and thinking what about me Dad? Where is my suddenly, I know you love me but why does the pain scream my name as I continue to point the blame to others for the tears on my face it should be her face because I have been saved, and delivered from the torment and nashing of the teeth. I am born, I confessed that I believe and receive your promises but then I turn and walk right back into the battle after I have already excepted you as my Father and Savior, and I left my pain and lies at the altar. Dad I need you daily, without you I am torn.

THE LIES YOU TELL

At a very young age I was given the gift to express myself through poems.

But at the same time lies were being whispered to me, that no one is listening, no one cares and that I was not good enough. For decades I believed this lie, that I had no voice and I was an orphan. In those Lies, I found depression, and endless tears of sorrow. I fell down many times, but found the strength to get right back up. I was stuck in strongholds when I did not even know what a stronghold was, I had soul ties when I had the desire to be free. I had anxiety when the word says be anxious for nothing. Then one day I received a revelation, that what I was going through was not how my life would turn out. I had to reach deep within myself and let go and let God be the author of my life if I wanted to see heaven here on earth. In my spirit, I heard that he has other plans for me and they are good. If I seek God with all my heart, when I go to him and pray he will hear me. The strongholds were broken and I began to see my self-worth as a daughter of the King, I was no longer an orphan I now have a father of the most high.

But God

I thought I was not worth his love, because at times I fall short
But God
I thought I cannot go to him and ask for forgiveness because I knew
better, and I did it anyway
But God
I remember not having enough food to eat and thinking where would
we get our next meal
But God
I remember the unselfish act of a woman who God sent to me as my
Godmother, as she took food from her freezer to place on our table
But God
I remember her teaching me how to pray and battle the enemy
But God
I remember as a teen, sleeping on the floor at a friend's house because
I no longer had a home of my own
But God
I had a child out of wedlock and thought, God would never bless me
again, he gives me grace
But God
I remember wanting another chance at marriage the right way and he
sent me Mr. Awesome
But God
I remember thinking I would not be blessed with another child, yet
he sent us an angel
But God

God is so good, he gives us more than we deserve. God is the way, the truth and the life. If we align ourselves with the word of God, he will give us the desires of our hearts because, they will be his desires for us.